Myths &
of the Peak

Roly Smith

Thor's Cave, Manifold Valley

MYTHS & LEGENDS OF THE PEAK

Introduction

In common with many remote upland areas, the Peak District attracts myths and legends as frequently as the mists which often cloak its hills. In many villages and farmhouses in these secret hills and dales, tales of the supernatural and the old, pre-Christian religion are still told, at times almost taking on a veneer of fact. And as these stories have been handed down from generation to generation, often growing in the telling, they have lost none of their original drama and intrigue.

Larger-than-life mythical characters such as Robin Hood and his faithful lieutenant Little John, and King Arthur and his Knights still stalk these hills, and are still remembered in ancient placenames, where their supernatural deeds were allegedly performed. Examples which recall the famous outlaw include Robin Hood's Stride, a strange, twin-towered gritstone outcrop near Winster (which is also known as Mock Beggar's Hall); Robin Hood's Cave, on Stanage Edge, and Robin Hood's Picking Rods, on Cown Edge above Chisworth. Little John is said to have been born in the village of Hathersage in the Hope Valley, and his alleged grave is shown to visitors just outside the south door of St Michael's Church.

And there's the mysterious chasm of Lud's Church, deep in the trees of Back Forest, near The Roaches, which has been identified as the Green Chapel in the early English Authurian alliterative poem *Sir Gawain and the Green Knight*.

Other mythical figures who are remembered in the Peakland landscape include the Norse god of thunder Thor, whose name is remembered in the yawning cave which overlooks the Manifold Valley in Staffordshire, and at haunted Odin Mine, under Mam Tor near Castleton, which was named after another Norse god and is said to be one of the oldest lead mines in the Peak.

Strangely, although the Peak District is about as far as you can get from the sea in these islands, there are several legends concerning mermaids and other mythical underwater creatures. They are supposed to emerge from the depths of murky moorland pools to trap the unwary at places like the two named Mermaid's Pools in the district, one on the western slopes of Kinder Scout and the other on lofty Morridge in the Staffordshire Moorlands.

Ghosts are still said to haunt some rooms in several of the Peak's ancient stone-built manor houses, and there are screaming skulls which vociferously object to being moved. Tales of murder and mayhem abound in what are now seemingly peaceful Peakland villages, like the story of Allan and Clara, cruelly murdered in the Winnats Pass, near Castleton. Ghostly, flickering lights are still seen in places like Longdendale, and phantom aircraft haunt the skies above aircrash sites on the high moors of the Dark Park, while mysterious, unexplained UFOs are regularly seen in the infamous Bonsall Triangle in the White Peak.

Come with us now as we embark on a journey of discovery and delve into some of the Peak District's most enduring myths and legends.

Tales of Arthur: Sir Gawain & the Green Knight and the Legend of Alderley Edge

Deep in the woodland of Back Forest, north west of The Roaches in the Staffordshire Moorlands is a mysterious mossy chasm still marked on some OS maps as "Lud's Church (cave)". Actually, it is not a cave at all, but a huge natural landslip in the gritstone bedrock, which has created a winding fissure about 60ft/18m deep and only 20ft/6m wide at the top, and largely hidden by the forest trees.

The name "Lud" supposedly comes from the fact that it was used for illegal services by Walter de Ludank, a Lollard follower of the religious reformer John Wycliffe, during the 16th century. The story goes that the secret natural chapel was raided by the King's troops, and Walter's daughter was accidently shot dead. For many years, a white statue (actually a ship's figurehead) supposed to represent Alice de Ludank stood high on the walls of the chasm, and she is still said to haunt the place.

But the legends of Lud's Church go back much further than that. One of the earliest poems in the English language is *Sir Gawain and the Green Knight*, a 14th century Authurian alliterative poem by an unknown author. This gory tale of beheadings sets Gawain's fateful rendezvous with the Green Knight in a Green Chapel. This was identified as Lud's Church during the 1960s by an academic from Keele University, based on the medieval poet's detailed description of the area, and the north Midland dialect in which it was written.

Another Arthurian legend associated with the western side of the Peak District is the legend of the Wizard of Alderley Edge, the wooded escarpment which overlooks the Cheshire Plain near Wilmslow. Alderley Edge is honeycombed with old copper, cobalt and lead mine workings some of which may date back as far as the Bronze Age.

Lud's Church, Back Forest

The Legend of Alderley, according to local author Alan Garner who was told it by his grandfather, relates to a farmer from Mobberley who was taking a white mare for sale at Macclesfield Fair. As he reached the cave known as Thieves' Hollow on Alderley Edge, he was approached by an old bearded man who said he wanted to buy the horse from him. The farmer thought he could get a better price at the fair, so he refused the sale.

The farmer failed to sell the horse in Maccesfield, and on the way home, met up with the old man again by Thieves' Hollow. He agreed the sale and then was led to Stormy Point, where the old man struck the rock with his staff. Miraculously, the rock opened up and the farmer was led inside through a pair of iron gates into a cave where slept King Arthur with 149 of his knights all in silver armour, alongside their 148 white horses. The farmer's white horse was obviously needed to make up the number.

The astonished farmer was paid for his horse with golden treasure and then taken back to the iron gates which closed behind him. Try as he might, he could never find it again.

Robin Hood & Little John – Stanage Edge & Hathersage

Some of the most common legends in the Peak concern England's most famous folk hero and outlaw Robin Hood, who, if place-names are anything to go by, was a frequent visitor to these Derbyshire hills.

Robin Hood's Stride, near Winster, is an amazing gritstone outcrop topped by two isolated pinnacles, about the length of a cricket pitch apart, indicating that the legendary outlaw must also have been a giant. An alternative name for the outcrop is Mock Beggar's Hall from its resemblance to a ruined building when seen from a distance, especially at dusk.

Robin Hood's faithful lieutenant, Little John was certainly a giant and allegedly born in Hathersage in the Hope Valley, where he was apprenticed as a nail-maker. You can still see his enormous grave, cared for by the Ancient Order of Foresters, between two stunted yews just outside the porch in the churchyard of St Michael's.

Nearby on the gritstone escarpment of Stanage Edge, Robin Hood's Cave has been a convenient bivouac for generations of rock climbers, and there are also Robin Hood's and Little John's Wells on the National Trust's nearby Longshaw estate, and a hamlet and pub called Robin Hood on the A619 Chesterfield road from Baslow.

Above & right: Little John's grave,
St Michael's, Hathersage

Below: Robin Hood's Stride

Mermaid's Pools – Kinder Scout & Morridge

Unlikely as it may seem being so far from the sea, there are several legends linked to mermaids inhabiting Peak District pools. Perhaps the best-known is the one haunting the dark, reed-fringed tarn known as Mermaid's Pool, which lies under the western shoulder of the Peak's highest point, the forbidding 2,000ft/ 600m plateau of Kinder Scout, above Hayfield.

The story goes that a beautiful mermaid lives in a cave on the side of Kinder and comes out every day to bathe in the pool. And the legend is that if you are lucky enough to see her on Easter Eve, you will be granted immortality. Before you dismiss such an unlikely occurrence, you should remember the story of the retired soldier Aaron Ashton of nearby Hayfield, who was a frequent visitor to the Mermaid's Pool and died in 1835 at the ripe old age of 104.

Over on the Staffordshire side of the Peak lies another moorland pool associated with a mermaid. The circular tarn known as Blake Mere lies close to the Mermaid Inn high on Morridge to the east of Leek, and is thought to be bottomless. A poem preserved in the pub warns visitors not to be tempted if the mermaid appears:

> She calls on you to greet her,
> Combing her dripping crown,
> And if you go to meet her,
> She ups and drags you down.

Jenny Greenteeth – Doxey Pool, The Roaches

Visible to the north from Blake Mere across the Leek–Buxton road you can see the serrated skyline of Ramshaw Rocks and the Roaches, which boast some of the most spectacular natural rock formations in the Peak.

Situated at over 1,500ft/450m on the Roaches ridge, with its far-reaching views across the Cheshire Plain towards the distant Mersey, lies another dark, deep peaty pool known as Doxey Pool. This harbours another legend of a mermaid with an equally fiercesome reputation as her counterpart at Blake Mere. But this one has a name – Jenny Greenteeth – and she appears to tempt passersby into the watery depths of Doxey Pool.

Indeed, the two murky pools are said to be connected, so perhaps it is the same mermaid, and both share the legend that they never seem to increase or decrease in size, and no birds are supposed to fly over them.

Hedessa & Hulac – Demon's Dale/Monsal Dale

A female human skull found recently on the banks of the River Wye in Bakewell evoked memories of the ancient folktale of Demon's Dale. The legend concerns the misdeeds of a giant known as Hulac Warren who lived in Demon's Dale, a couple of miles upstream from the find site. Hulac abducted a beautiful local shepherdess called Hedessa, but when he tried to force his attentions on her she resisted.

In the ensuing struggle, she fell to her death on the bank of the River Wye at a spot where a spring now rises – the pure, warm spring waters representing Hedessa's tears. For his heinous crime, Hulac was turned into a weathered crag of limestone, which still lies mid–stream in the Wye and is known as The Warren Stone.

The Battle of Win and Lose Hills

The twin sentinels of Lose Hill 1,563ft/476m and Win Hill 1,518ft/462m guard the entrance to Edale from the Hope Valley, and were the scene of a legendary Dark Age battle, sometime in the seventh century.

Cuicholm, king of Wessex and Edwin, king of Northumbria were embroiled in a dispute over land boundaries, and Cuicholm had sent an envoy to the court of Edwin with instructions to murder the king. However, the plot was foiled by the heroic intervention of Lilla, one of Edwin's chief thegns, who died as a result of his wounds, and is commemorated by Lilla Cross high on the North York Moors.

Intent on revenge, Edwin marched south and reached the Peak where Cuicholm had amassed a huge army which was swelled by the forces of Penda, king of Mercia, another implacable enemy of Edwin. The two opposing armies camped overnight on the twin hills at the entrance to Edale, and when they met the following day, somewhere near the present Townhead Bridge, the River Noe was said to have run red with the blood of the fallen.

Local tradition has it that Edwin's winning forces had camped on 'Win' Hill the night before, while Cuicholm's losers, had chosen 'Lose' Hill, so the result was a foregone conclusion. Despite the fact that placename evidence tells us that Win Hill gets its name from the withies (an old name for rowans) which still grow upon it, and Lose Hill (pronounced 'loose') means the hill of the pig sties, many local people still seem to prefer the old story.

Win Hill (centre) with Lose Hill to the right

The legend of Eldon Hole – Peak Forest

Eldon Hole, the Peak's largest open pothole on the south side of Eldon Hill above Peak Forest, was long thought to be bottomless. When Daniel Defoe toured the Peak in the 18th century, it was one of the few "Wonders of the Peak" he actually thought was impressive, describing it as "a frightful chasm" which was a mile deep!

The legend of Eldon Hole is that when a goose was once thrown into the hole, it eventually emerged a few days later from Peak Cavern in Castleton, its feathers apparently singed by the fires of Hell. And when local landowner the Earl of Leicester decided to test its depths, he apparently lowered a local peasant down who, when hauled back to the surface, had become a gibbering, white-haired idiot.

The first recorded descent into Eldon Hole was by John Lloyd in 1770, who found it was not bottomless after all, and measured its depth as about 270ft/82m. It was probably once much deeper than that, but generations of passers by have thrown rocks into the gaping void, building up the bottom level.

Eldon Hole,
near Peak Forest

The Bakewell Witches

The pleasant market town of Bakewell, 'capital' of the Peak District, is probably best-known for its almond-flavoured dessert puddings, which are now exported all over the world.

But in the early 17th century, at the height of James I's purge on witches, it was the scene of an alleged example of witchcraft which involved the transportation of a man from Bakewell to the heart of faraway London.

The story goes that a Scotsman was lodging with a Mrs Stafford in Bakewell when he was awoken in the middle of the night by the sound of chanting in the room beneath. He heard Mrs Stafford and her accomplice, possibly her sister, chanting:

Over thick, over thin,
Now devil to the cellar in London

Mystified, he went back to bed and repeated the rhyme to himself and suddenly found himself whisked away through the air over the countryside to eventually end up, dishevelled and disorientated, in a cellar in a London warehouse alongside Mrs Stafford and her sister.

He was arrested on suspicion of intended robbery, and recounted his incredible story to the magistrate, claiming that if proof were needed, if they searched the house in Bakewell his belongings would be found. The magistrate, suspecting witchcraft, ordered a search to be made, and the Scotsman's belongings were duly found. The two women were accused of witchcraft and executed at Derby in 1607.

Lover's Leaps – Stoney Middleton and Dovedale

A former climbers' and cavers' café in Stoney Middleton, still sadly missed, had the intriguing name of the Lover's Leap. It got its name because it sheltered under an overhanging limestone crag where jilted lover Hannah Badderley unsuccessfully tried to commit suicide in 1762. She was saved by her voluminous skirt, which acted as a kind of parachute and wafted her gently to the ground.

Another Lover's Leap is to be found at the southern end of Dovedale, where a set of steps supposedly built by Italian prisoners of war during the Second World War climbs steadily up to a bare limestone promontory, which affords a wonderful view down the length of the dale.

Lover's Leap, Dovedale

The story here is that a young woman who believed her lover had been killed in the Napoleonic Wars threw herself off the top of the rocks, but just like Hannah Baddeley, her flapping skirts caught in the branches of a tree as she fell and saved her life. Thankfully, when she got home she heard that her boyfriend was alive and well.

Peak Forest's Gretna Green

Peak Forest, a bleak village high on the White Peak plateau on the A623 east of Whaley Bridge, was once known by a quirk of ecclesiastical law as 'the Gretna Green of the Peak.'

The unusual dedication of the parish church of King Charles the Martyr gives a clue to its extra-parochial powers, for the original church was built in 1657 by the wife of the 2nd Earl of Devonshire during the time of the Commonwealth's ban on church building – thus falling outside the law. This meant that the priest was able to conduct marriages without question and at any time.

The situation continued until early in the 19th century, earning successive incumbents considerable sums of money. Couples can still be married in the church without banns being read, providing that one of the couple has lived in the village for 15 days prior to the ceremony. The present imposing Victorian church was built on the site of the old chapel in 1878.

The Winnats Murder – Castleton

Another foul deed which has entered into legend is the murder and robbery of Allan and Clara in the Winnats Pass, just outside Castleton (see cover photograph), in 1758. In mid-April of that year, the couple eloped against Clara's father's wishes, intending to get married at Peak Forest, Derbyshire's equivalent of Gretna Green.

They were on the final stage of their journey, through the Winnats Pass and then to Peak Forest via Eldon Hill and Sparrowpit when five drunken lead miners leapt out on them and robbed and then murdered them with their pick axes. When Allan and Clara were missed, local people suspected the worst, but it was to be many years later before their bodies were found and re-buried in St Edmund's churchyard at Castleton. But the identity of their murderers remained a mystery until a series of apparently accidental events pointed the finger at the five guilty men.

One of the miners bought horses with his share of the booty, but they all died in rapid succession. People began to put two and two together when the daughter of another of the miners was seen at church wearing a very rich silk dress. Some years after the deed, another of the guilty men fell from a precipice in the Winnats and was killed instantly, while another was mysteriously killed by a falling stone in the same place. A third lost his reason and died in a pitiful state, having tried to commit suicide on several occasions, and a fourth man was more successful in his death wish, and hanged himself.

Finally, the horse-owning miner, after lying on his death bed for 10 weeks, eventually owned up to the crime, and finally admitted that it was he and his four friends who had robbed, murdered and buried Allan and Clara.

Dorothy Vernon – Haddon Hall

Visitors to the attractive medieval fortified manor of Haddon Hall, on the banks of the River Wye just south of Bakewell, are still told the story of Dorothy Vernon. They are shown the steps down which she supposedly eloped and the bridge she crossed to make her assignment with John Manners, son of the Earl of Rutland.

Quite why her father, Sir George Vernon, the so-called King of the Peak, would object to his daughter making a very financially-rewarding marriage to the son of the Earl of Rutland, is not explained. And the fact that the steps from the Long Gallery and the packhorse bridge across the Wye were not built until long after Dorothy's death, also remains unexplained.

The truth is that the whole thing is a Victorian melodramatic invention, apparently first set down in W E Doubleday's *Heiress of Haddon* published at the turn of the century, and later even immortalised in the 1892 Arthur Sullivan operetta, *Haddon Hall*, with words by Sydney Grundy.

Lost Lad and Tip – Derwent Edge

A lofty 1,700ft/518m spur of Derwent Edge, below Back Tor in the wild Upper Derwent Valley has the strange name on the OS map of Lost Lad. This recalls an ancient legend that this was the wild and remote spot where a shepherd boy, lost in a fierce winter storm below the edge, finally crawled to seek shelter. He had scratched the words "Lost Lad" on the stones of the cairn which crowns the hilltop when his body was found weeks later.

The Upper Derwent is no stranger to such tales. A memorial by the side of the Derwent Dam in the valley below commemorates Tip, a sheepdog owned by Joseph Tagg, a local retired shepherd, who was lost on the moors during the winter of 1953-54. When his 86-year-old master succumbed to the blizzard, the faithful Tip stayed by his master's side until he was found 15 weeks later.

Derwent Edge

Eagle Stone – Baslow Edge

Ancient beliefs and legends are often associated with prehistoric remains or prominent natural features in the Peak, as with other upland areas.

One of these is the isolated eroded tor known as the Eagle Stone which stands on Baslow Edge. Local folklore claim that when the cock crows, it turns around, and that any young man wanting the hand of a maiden in Baslow would first have to show his mettle by climbing to the top of the stone.

The name of the Eagle Stone probably has nothing to do with the king of the birds. The most likely interpretation is that it derives from the Egglestone, or witches' stone; or maybe the pagan god Aigle, a giant who was adept at picking up large stones and throwing them over considerable distances.

Fair Flora – Grindleford

The forlorn marble statue of Flora, the Greek goddess of flowers, stands deep in the woodlands above Grindleford, apparently a monument to lost love.

The statue originally came from Chatsworth and was given by the Duke of Devonshire to the Bridgeman family of nearby Stoke Hall. There are several stories as to how the statue came to be where it is, the most common being that it was raised to the memory of a girl who was murdered by a jealous lover.

Another is that when the statue was taken to Stoke Hall, a series of misfortunes befell the hall and its occupants, and it was finally relegated out of sight in the woods. Yet another claims it was a memorial to a young girl who drowned in the swollen waters of the Derwent while she was eloping with her lover across the stepping stones above Leadmill Bridge, near Hathersage.

But no one can really know the truth now as to how Fair Flora came to be forgotten and abandoned among the trees of Stoke Wood.

Dickie's Skull – Tunstead

Dickie o'Tunstead is a disembodied skull which resided at Tunstead Farm, tucked under the escarpment of Ladder Hill overlooking the Combs Reservoir near Chapel-en-le-Frith.

No one knows for sure who Dickie was, and 'he' may have been taken from one of the many prehistoric barrows, or 'lows', on the hillside above the farm. The most common story is that he was a Tunstead man called Ned Dickson, who fought in France during the Huguenot Wars of the 16th century. On his return home to Tunstead Farm, he found that his cousin and his wife had given him up for dead, married, and claimed possession of the farm.

The couple were obviously not pleased to see Ned, but they invited him to spend the night at the farm. According to local tradition, they murdered him in his bed that night and secretly buried him on the farm, hoping no one would suspect what had happened.

But then things started to go wrong for the guilty couple, as they had for Allan and Clara's murderers in the Winnats Pass. They were haunted by strange and unexplained noises, illness and the failure of their crops. The hauntings came to a head when on a winter night less than a year after the murder, the dead man's head appeared to the terrified couple.

Eventually retribution struck the guilty couple. She was killed when her husband hit her, and he died when an ancient oak tree growing on the farm unexplicably fell down on him. The legend of Dickie's head is that while it is left where it is, it will protect the owners, but woe betide anyone who attempts to remove it. When the skull is removed, weird sounds, screams and disembodied voices haunt the house, and there is no rest for the occupants.

It was once taken to be buried in a Chapel churchyard, but the basket in which it was being carried got heavier and heavier as it was taken further away from the farm. On another occasion, it was thrown into Combs Reservoir, and all the fish in it mysteriously died.

Dickie was even claimed to be responsible for holding up the mighty London and North Eastern Railway. The line through the Combs Valley was planned to pass across land belonging to Tunstead Farm, but after an embankment was constructed and a bridge built to carry the road to the farm across the railway, the bridge sank into the ground and its stonework was dislodged. Eventually a new and expensive road and bridge had to be constructed into the Combs Valley, well away from the farm.

Dickie is not the only skull which acts as a good luck charm in some older Peak District houses. Another was traditionally kept on a window sill at Dunscar Farm, on the slopes running up to Mam Tor near Castleton, and yet another is well-documented high on the White Peak plateau at Flagg Hall, even being accepted as part of the house's valuation.

Highlow Hall ghosts – near Hathersage

Said to be one of Derbyshire's most haunted buildings, the delightfully contradictory Highlow Hall (now a private hotel) stands on the hills above Hathersage. Highlow Hall was the seat of Nicholas Eyre, of the famous Hope Valley dynasty, who married in 1340. He rejected one sister in favour of a younger one, and the aggrieved lady promptly committed suicide.

It is her ghost – the so-called "white lady" – which is said to haunt the building and who laid a curse on Nicholas and his family for 14 generations. The Eyres were major landowners in the Hope Valley, and the patriach of the family, Robert Eyre, the builder of the first Highlow Hall, came to England with the Conqueror. He was said to have constructed seven halls for his sons – all of which were visible from the others.

One of those other Eyre halls was Moorseats Hall, near Abney, which interestingly has its own ghost of another "white lady."

Haunted Highlow Hall

The Longdendale Lights

The most famous unexplained illuminations in the Peak District are the so-called Longdendale Lights. Longdendale crosses some of the highest and wildest moorland in the Peak District, between the 2,000ft/600m summits of Bleaklow and Black Hill. The valley floor is crammed with five reservoirs; the busy A628 Woodhead trunk road between Sheffield and Manchester; strings of ugly electricity pylons; and a former railway line, now used as the Longdendale Trail.

The Longdendale Lights – locally known as 'the Devil's Bonfires' – have been seen haunting the gritstone cloughs on the northern face of Bleaklow for generations. They seem to be concentrated around the hairpin bend known as the Devil's Elbow on the minor road from Glossop, to the short, steep-sided valley appropriately known as Shining Clough at the eastern end of the valley, or around the strange isolated natural mound to the north west of Bleaklow summit known as Torside Castle.

The lights take the form of powerful beams and pulsating balls of coloured lights sweeping across the northern gritstone escarpment of Bleaklow and all along the escarpment from Bramah Edge to Shining Clough. They've been seen by local people for many years, but also by the emergency services such as the police and mountain rescue teams, which are often called out to investigate what appears to be a plane crash or accident on the moors.

The source remains a mystery. Theories include lights from airliners approaching Manchester Airport, ball lightning, marsh gases or 'will o' the wisps', or even electrical discharges from the pylons which stride down the valley. But none of the explanations can account for the range of light phenomena seen in Longdendale. Now there's even a heavily-visited website which is dedicated to the Lights, with a webcam constantly trained, 24-hours-a-day, on the valley.

Many of the other strange lights in the sky can be simply explained, of course, as aircraft lights or meteorological ballons. Others have been described as Unidentified Atmospheric Phenomena (or UAPs), such as the little-understood natural electromagnetic forces which can create glowing energy fields.

But just as mysterious are the reports of Unidentified Flying Objects (UFOs) which are regularly and increasingly seen in certain areas of the Peak District. The area around the White Peak village of Bonsall – the so-called 'Bonsall Triangle' – seems to be particularly attractive to these weird and unexplained lights in the skies.

Most of them take the form of bright lights seen at night, which in some cases follow cars with a spotlight to the terror of their occupants, while some – silvery metallic in appearance – have even allegedly been seen to land.

The Legend of Over Exposed, Higher Shelf Stones, Bleaklow

Over 50 aircraft wrecks litter the Dark Peak moors, and they have claimed the lives of about 200 pilots and crew since the Second World War.

One of the most famous is the USAF B-29 Superfortress *Over Exposed* on Higher Shelf Stones, the south-western buttress of 2,076ft/633m Bleaklow and a prominent landmark to motorists as they drop down into Glossop after crossing the notorious Snake Pass.

Over Exposed had played an important role in photographing the first atomic bomb tests over Bikini Atoll in the South Pacific in 1946, and was also used on photo reconnaisance missions over Russian-occupied East Germany during the Berlin Airlift.

In November, 1948, *Over Exposed* was part of the 16th Photographic Reconnaisance Squadron, Strategic Air Command, stationed at the former Dambusters' base at RAF Scampton in Lincolnshire. *Over Exposed's* young crew, led by the 33-year-old Captain Langdon P Tanner, were in a happy mood because they had just completed their service overseas, and were due to return home to the US in three days' time.

A routine flight had been scheduled for them to take the payroll to the USAF staff at RAF Burtonwood, near Warrington. What happened next, no one can be sure. But 20 minutes into the 25-minute flight, *Over Exposed* crashed into the peat just to the north of the 2,000-foot/600m summit of Higher Shelf Stones and burst into flames. All 13 crew members were killed outright.

There is still a surprising amount of the Superfortress left at the crash site, including the remains of the four Wright Cyclone engines and bits of Perspex, twisted steel and aluminium, along with a plaque and poppies left by local people.

Sometime in the early Seventies, an aviation historian from Glossop had been at the wreck site and uncovered what he thought was a brass washer. When he cleaned it, he was astonished to find it was a gold wedding ring, inscribed with the name of the captain of the doomed aircraft – Langdon P Tanner.

Soon after his discovery, he took a party of enthusiasts to the site to show them where he had made the find. "I bent down to show them where I found the ring and when I looked up, they had scarpered and were 10 to 15 yards away," he recalled later. "When I caught up with them they were ashen-faced. They said they had seen someone standing behind me, looking down and dressed in full flying uniform."

Ghostly Dambusters – Upper Derwent Valley

Stories of phantom aircraft, air crashes and ghostly airmen are not uncommon at or around wreck sites on the Dark Peak moors. Among the most common of these are the tales of people seeing low-flying Avro Lancaster bombers over the Derwent moors, or the Ladybower, Derwent or Howden Reservoirs in the Upper Derwent Valley.

The Derwent Valley was one of several sites throughout Britain which were used by Wing Commander Guy Gibson's legendary 617 Squadron – the Dambusters – during their brief period of training before their epic raid on the Ruhr dams in 1943. In fact, very few flights were made over the Derwent Dams and certainly none of Barnes Wallis's famous 'bouncing bombs' were ever dropped there.

The valley's superficial resemblance to the steep, wooded valleys of the Ruhr, and the twin towers on the Derwent and Howden Dams (the Ladybower Dam was then still under construction) to the German Moehne and Eder Dams, made it the perfect location to practice the necessary low-level flying skills required.

Following a series of very popular reunions and flypasts on the site in the 1980s, all new pilots of the present 617 Squadron apparently make their maiden flights in their Tornado jets over the valley. The Derwent Valley was also the scene for the still-popular and often-repeated 1955 film of *The Dambusters,* starring Michael Redgrave as Barnes Wallis and Richard Todd as Guy Gibson. Such is the legend of the film and its even more memorable theme march by Eric Coates. Richard Todd was invited to be the guest of honour at the most-recent reunion and flypast by the last surviving flying Lancaster PA 474, *City of Lincoln,* in 1993.

Although none of the Lancasters was lost in these training flights (unlike on the actual raid, when eight out of 19 aircraft did not return and 53 aircrew out of 133 lost their lives), ghostly figures of airmen have been reported around the Derwent Dam, and low-flying Lancasters have consistently been reported sighted over the moors around.

A Lancaster bomber flying over the Derwent Dams to commemorate the 65th anniversary of the epic raid on the Ruhr dams in 1943

Then there is the story of the farmer who collected some possibly usable pieces of wreckage from a downed Bristol Blenheim bomber on Sykes Moor near Glossop. He took them back to his farm and stored them in a barn. But soon afterwards, he and his son were astonished to see the barn 'almost shake itself to pieces'. They immediately took the wreckage back to the crash site, and the hauntings stopped.

In March, 1997, police and emergency services were called out after a number of independent callers had reported a low-flying plane described by eye-witnesses as being 'like an old wartime Lancaster' apparently crashing into the bleak moors at the head of Howden Reservoir in the middle of the night. Several farmers and gamekeepers saw the aircraft, and reported hearing a huge explosion as the aircraft apparently hit the ground.

A full call-out of the mountain rescue services ensued, with over 100 volunteers, search and rescue dogs and two helicopters searching more than 40 square miles of some of the wildest and most inaccessible moorland in the Peak. The intensive operation was eventually called off after 15 hours of exhaustive but ultimately fruitless searching. No trace of any kind of crash could be found, and the event remains a complete mystery.

BIBLIOGRAPHY

Alderley Edge and its Neighbourhood (J Swinnerton, 1843, reprinted by EJ Morten, 1972)

Sir Gawain and the Green Knight trans. by Brian Stone (Penguin, 1959)

Legends of Derbyshire by John Merrill (Dalesman,1972)

Derbyshire Traditions by Clarence Daniel (Dalesman, 1975)

Ghosts of Derbyshire by Clarence Daniel (Dalesman, 1977)

Ghosts and Legends of the Peak District by David Clarke (Jarrold,1991)

Supernatural Peak District by David Clarke (Robert Hale, 2000)

Murder and Mystery in the Peak by Roly Smith (Halsgrove, 2004)

Acknowledgements

Photography

© **Mark Titterton** Front cover; p.2; p.5; p.7middle; p.8-9; p.10; p.14; p.16; p.19
© **Edward Rokita** p.7top & bottom; P.11
© **Courtesy of The Peak District Mining Museum** p.12
© **Peter Bailey** p.23

Special thanks to
The Peak District Mining Museum – www.peakmines.co.uk

Published by **Ashbourne Editions**
10 Queen Elizabeth Court, Belle Vue Road, Ashbourne DE6 1NE
Tel: (01335) 344882 Mobile: 07890 854634

1st edition: ISBN: 978-1-873-775-44-8

Printed
Gomer Press, Llandysul, Wales

Design
www.ceibagraphics.co.uk